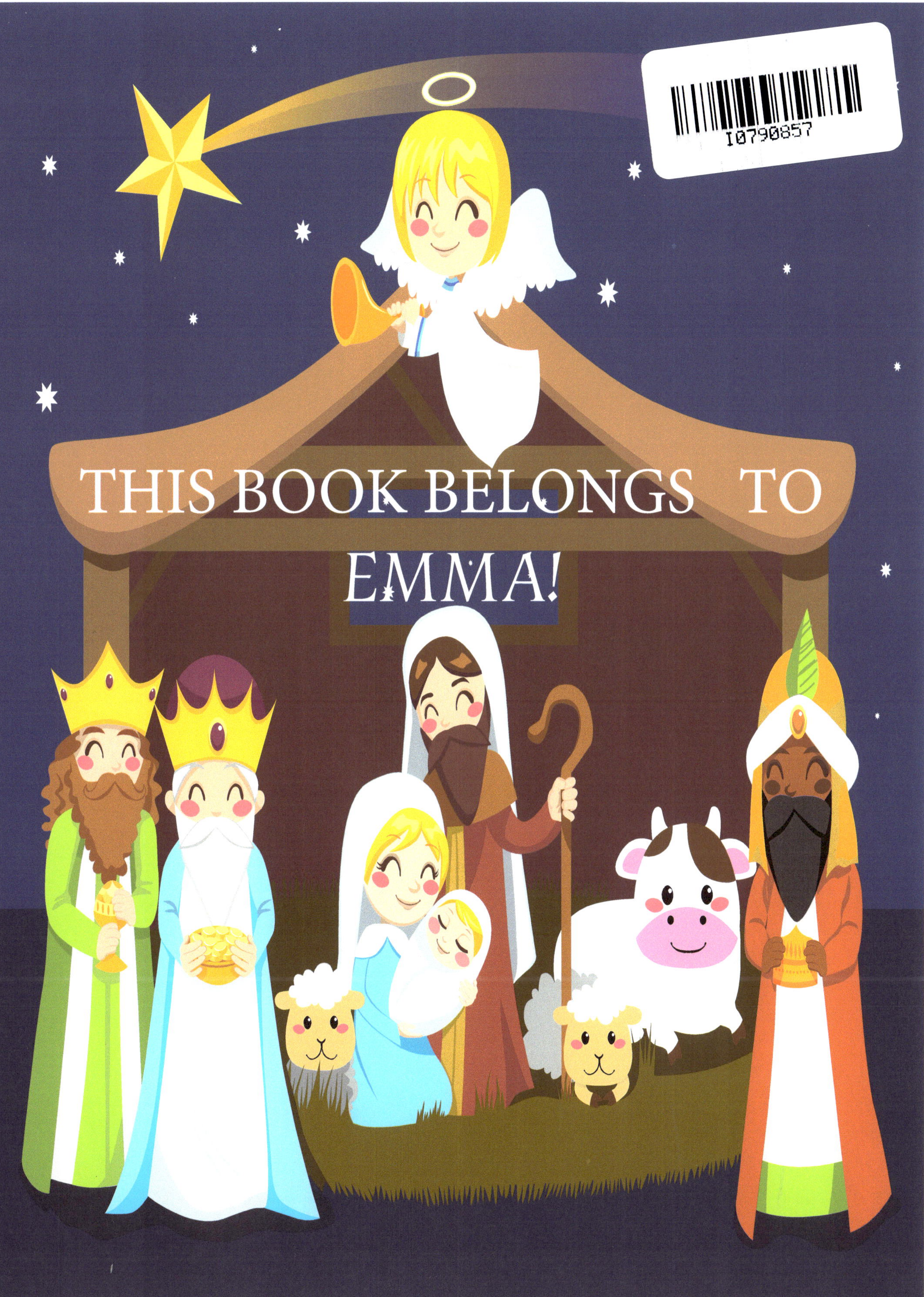
THIS BOOK BELONGS TO
EMMA!
I0790857

Tips for Using this Book:

1. You will need these supplies to get started: scissors, glue, dice, crayons, markers, or colored pencils, game board pieces, and extra paper.

2. Color in each day on the calendar as you complete the activity. Then glue the days in the correct order on another sheet of paper.

3. At the end of the book, extra pictures have been included for your nativity scenes.

4 You are free to do the book in any order because some activities/games may take more time to finish.

5. Have fun with family or friends as you do the activities and play the board games!

Advent Calendar

DAY 1

Cut and glue the pieces to create a nativity scene.

DAY 2

Name or make a list of the 10 things that don't belong in the scene.

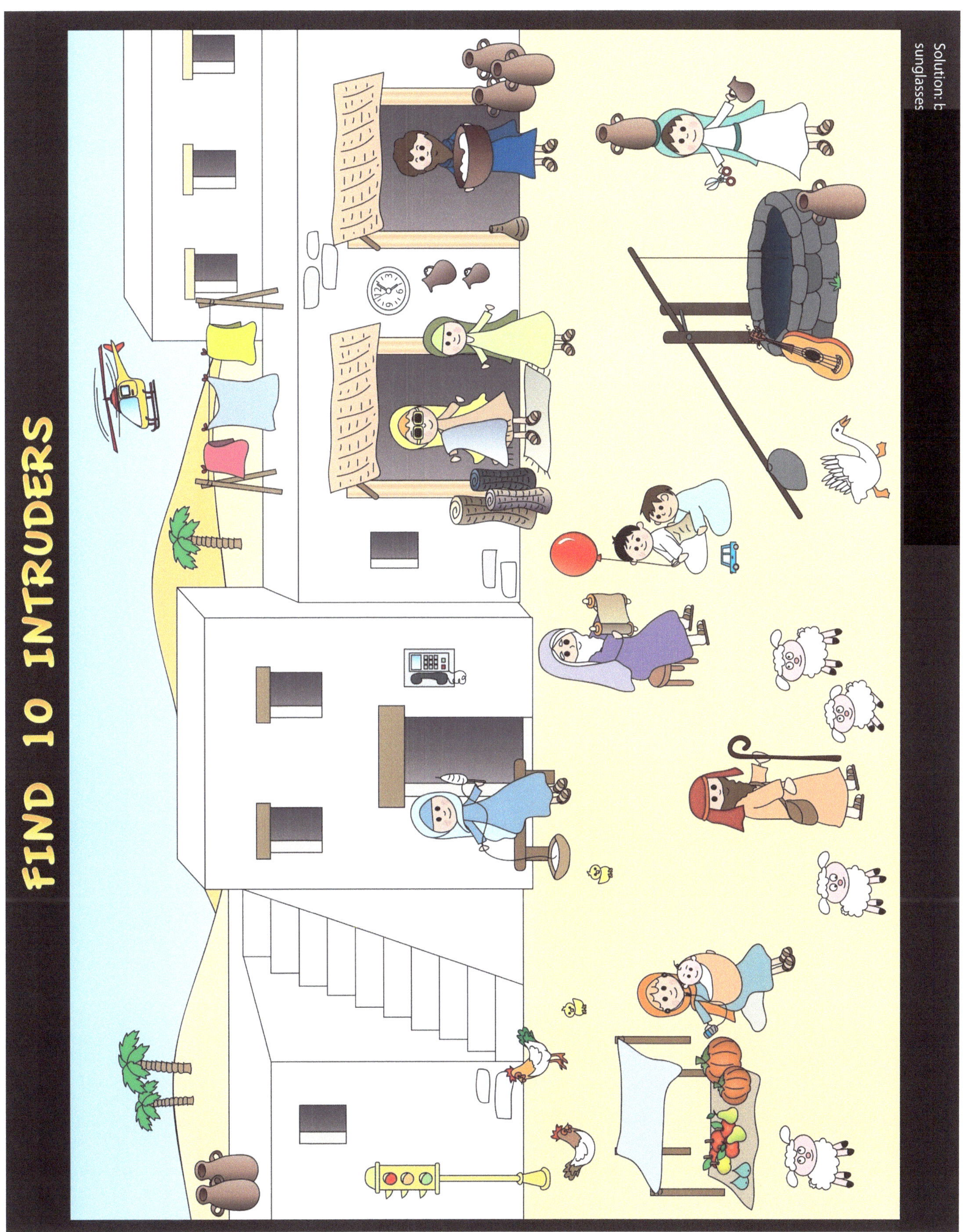

DAY 3

Emma, help the angel find baby Jesus! Should she follow maze 1, 2, or 3?

DAY 4

Find the words in the word search to reveal the mystery word.

N	A	T	I	V	I	T	Y	M	S
S	J	K	I	N	G	S	S	L	T
A	O	O	B	B	E	T	H	A	A
M	X	C	S	I	H	L	E	P	R
T	Y	A	T	E	B	E	E	L	Y
S	R	M	T	E	P	L	P	E	E
I	A	E	U	H	M	H	E	G	K
R	M	L	H	E	G	O	D	N	N
H	J	E	S	U	S	M	C	A	O
C	D	R	E	H	P	E	H	S	D

DAY 5

How are the two pictures different? Name them or make a list of the differences on another sheet of paper.

DAY 6

Cut out and glue the game board pieces. Take turns rolling the dice to see who gets to the manger first.

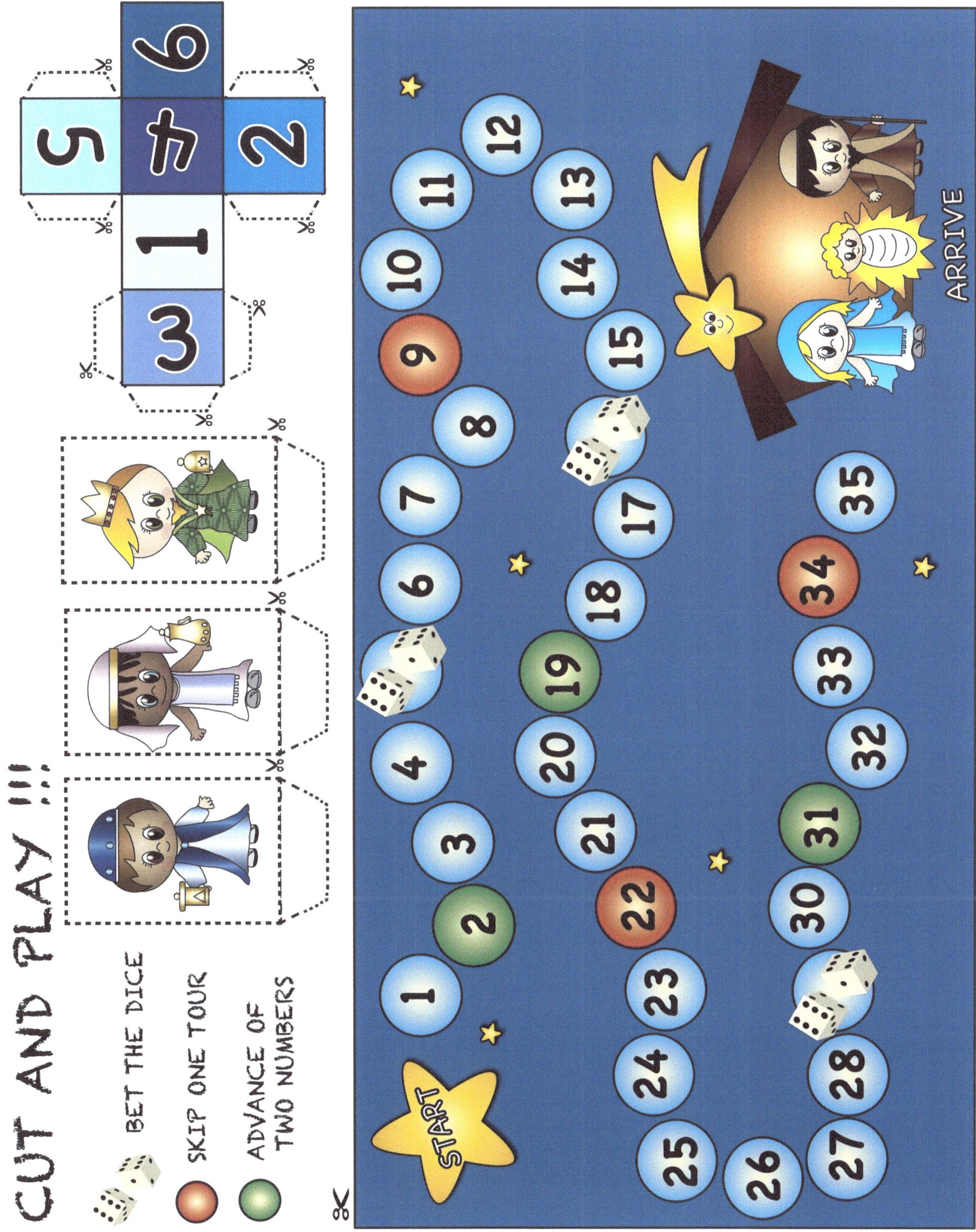

DAY 7

Emma, the Three Wise Men are lost! Help them each choose the correct maze.

DAY 8

How are the two pictures different?
Name them or make a list of the differences on paper.

FIND THE TEN DIFFERENCES

DAY 9

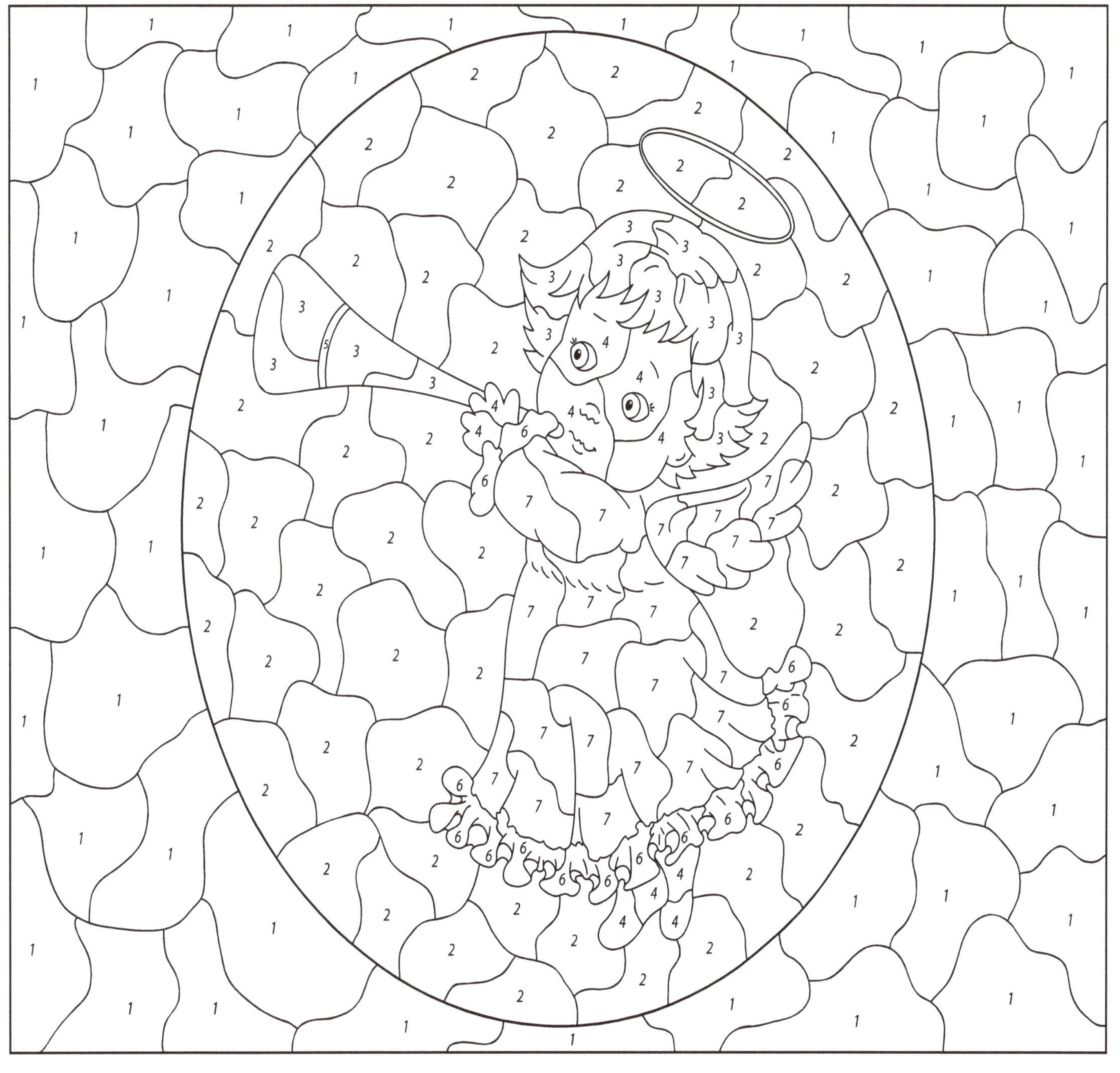

Emma,
Color by number to
finish the
Christmas angel.

DAY 10

Cut and glue the pieces. You may use them for your nativity scenes or game boards.

DAY 11

Help the shepherd & his sheep choose the correct maze. Should he take A, B, C, or D?

DAY 12

Roll the dice to find out how many spaces you move on the game board. Use the game board to practice counting, too!

DAY 13

Emma, cut out the pictures and glue them to the numbered pictures.

DAY 14

Roll the dice to find out how many spaces you move on the game board. Use the game board to practice counting, too!

DAY 15

How are the two pictures different?
Name them or make a list of the differences on paper.

DAY 16

Cut out & glue the game board pieces then follow the directions at the bottom of the page.

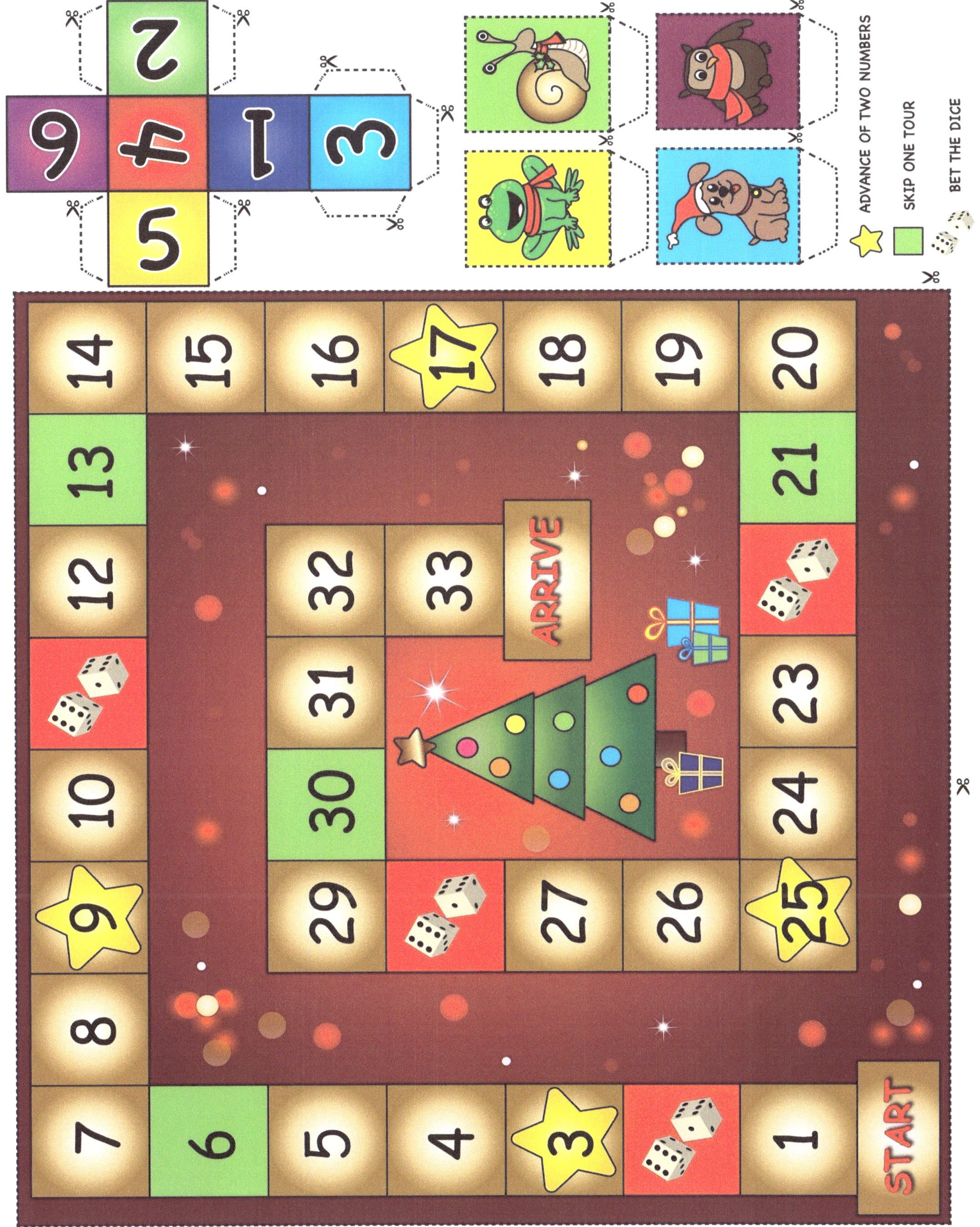

DAY 17

Write the word for each numbered picture. Decide if the word goes down or across. Hint: Count the number of spaces to help you decide where the word fits.

DAY 18

Add the total number of ornaments from both of the trees. Decorate the
blank tree with the total number of ornaments by using
colored pencils, markers,gel pens, or crayons.

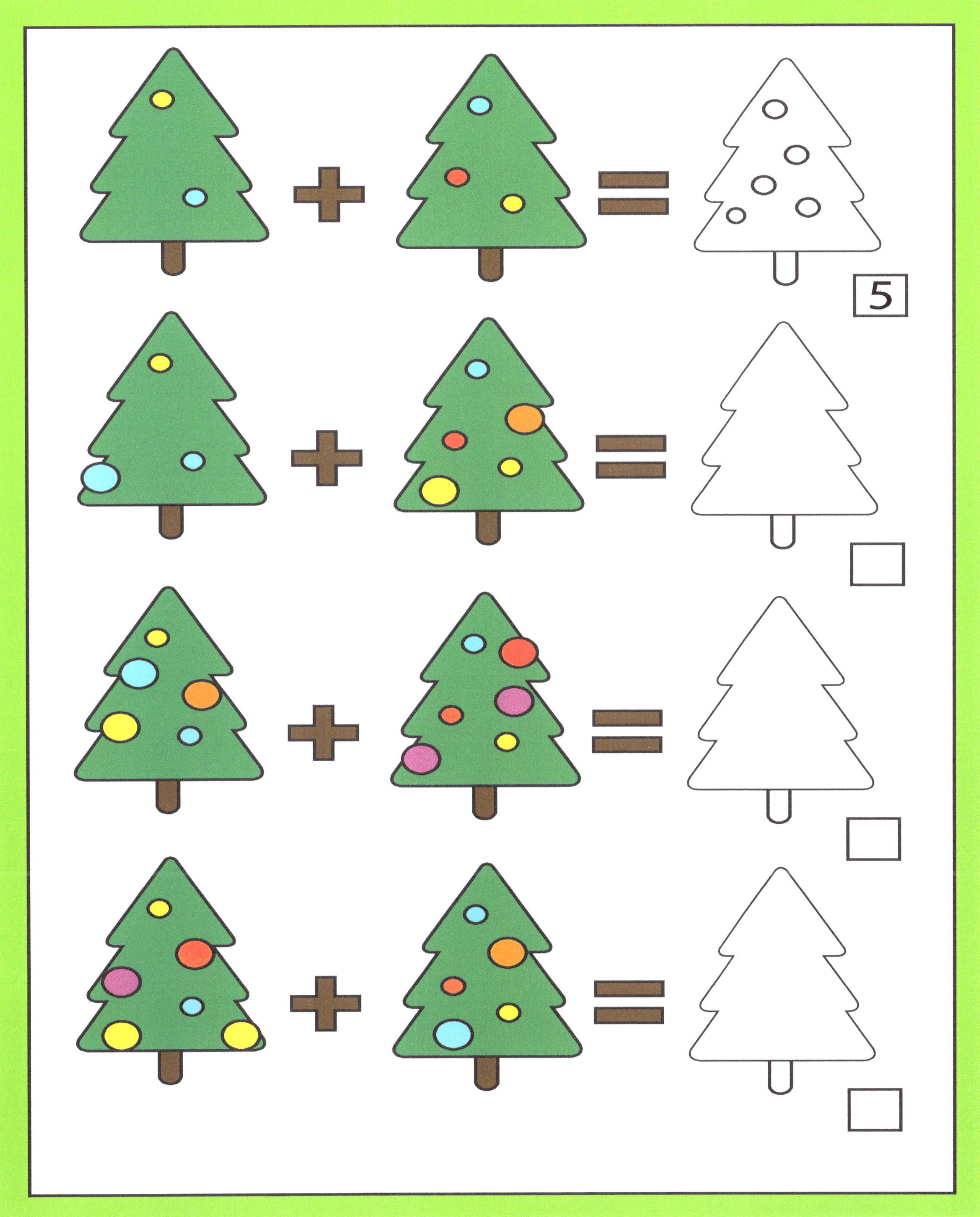

DAY 19

Help the Three Wise Men choose the correct maze to find baby Jesus.

Jesus.

DAY 20

Color by number to decorate the Christmas tree!

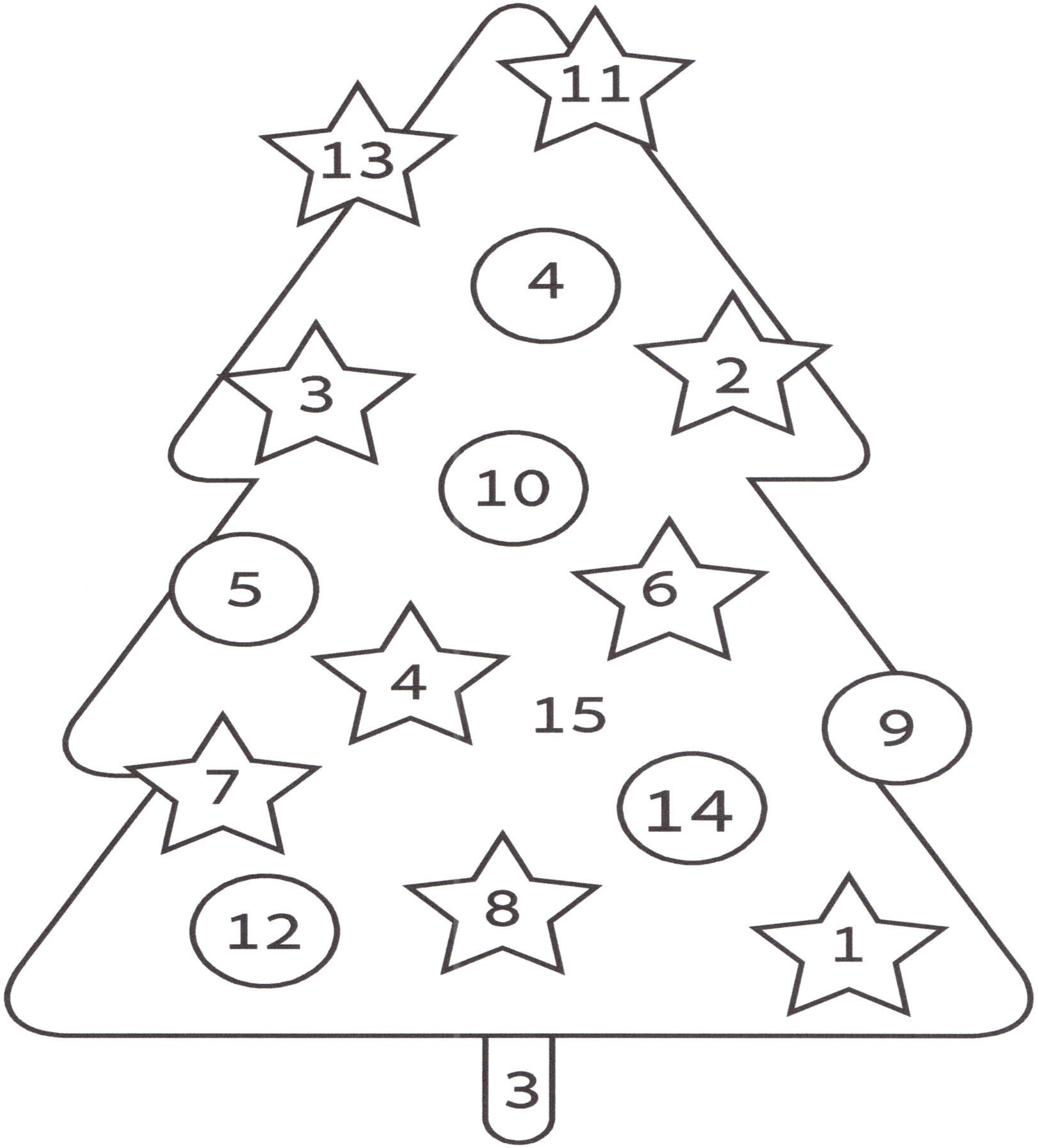

1 blue
2 grey
3 brown
4 yellow
5 pink
6 purple
7 indigo
8 orange
9 black
10 nude
11 red
12 golden
13 silver
14 lilac
15 green

DAY 21

Cut out and glue the game board pieces. Then follow the directions at the top of the page.

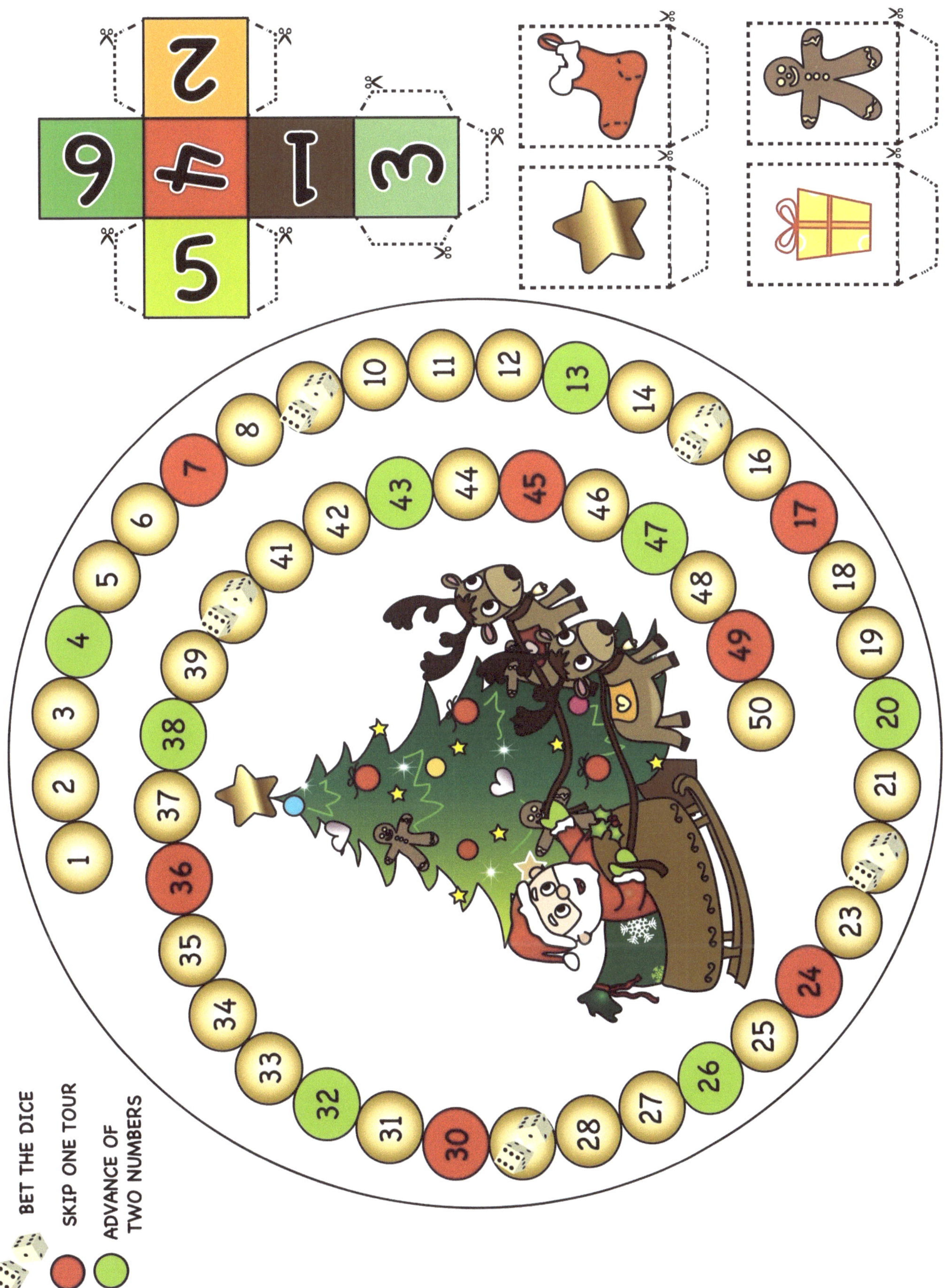

DAY 22

Christmas word search
As you find the words in the word search, color the letters with a crayon, marker, gel pen, or colored pencils.

s f i r e p l a c e
t b e h c a n d y c
a o l a s a n t a a
r x f t b a l l n n
c a n d l e h r g e
g i n g e r b r e a
m i t t e n s l l d
s n o w f l a k e m
b e l l s t r e e a
r e i n d e e r a n

1. Angel
2. Ball
3. Bells
4. Box
5. Candle
6. Candy cane
7. Elf
8. Fireplace
9. Gingerbread man
10. Hat
11. Mittens
12. Reindeer
13. Santa
14. Snowflake
15. Star
16. Tree

DAY 23

Compare the number of things found in each row.

Math Game

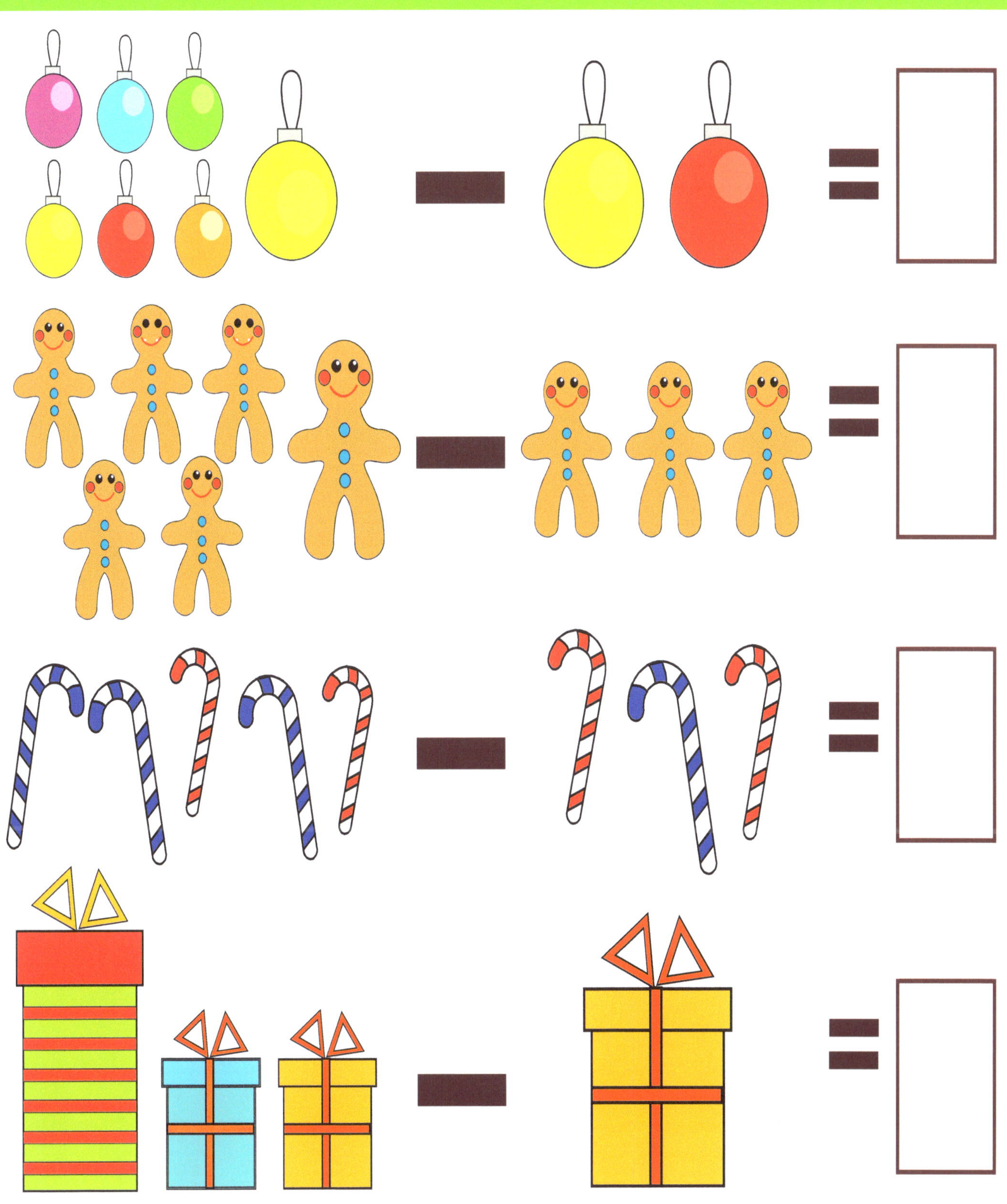

DAY 24

What do the letters spell in this maze?

DAY 25

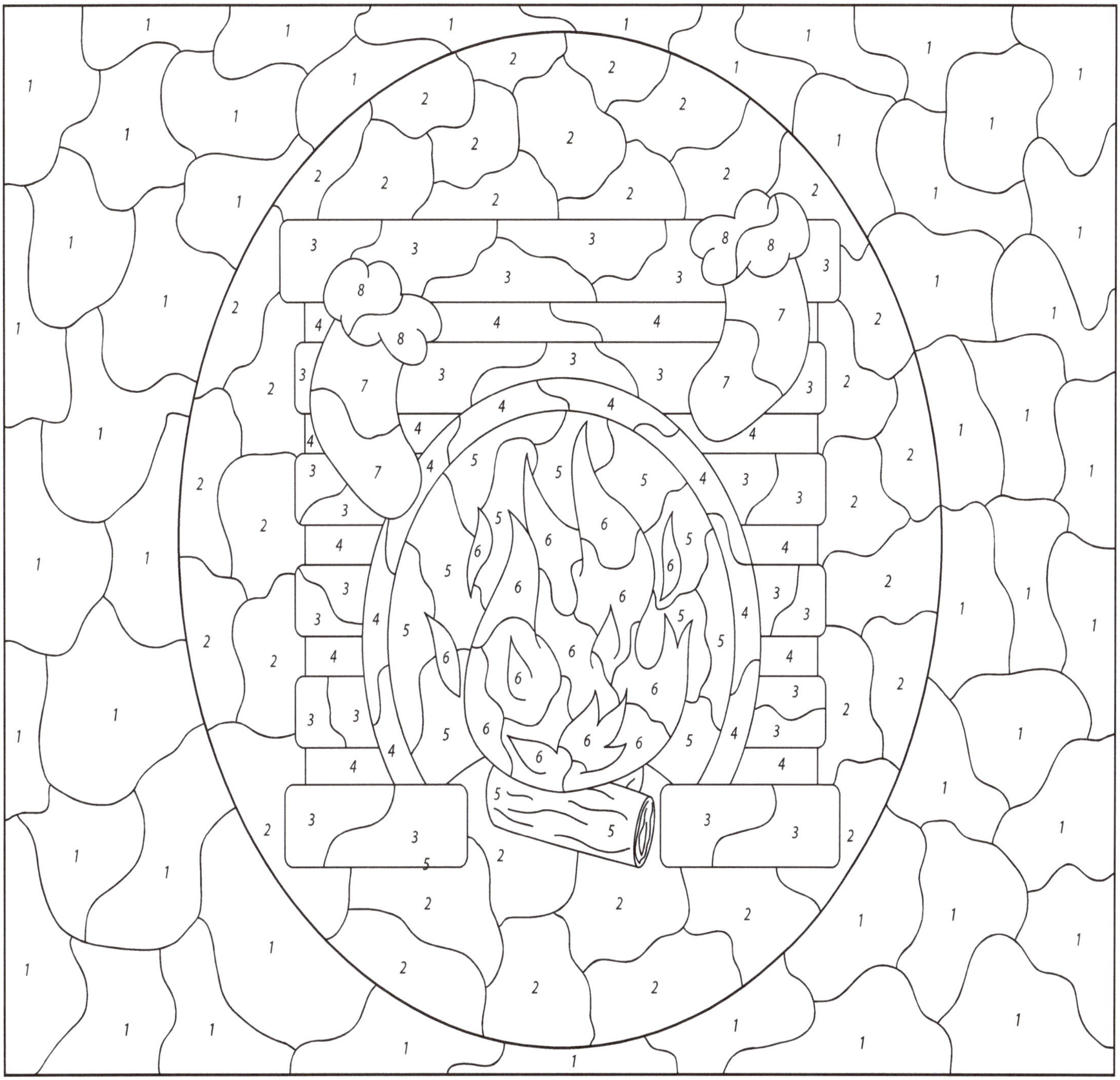

Color by number
to decorate the
holiday fireplace.

Emma, A bonus page for you!

C	S	R	E	B	M	E	C	E	D
C	H	R	I	B	B	O	N	W	E
A	A	R	Y	R	R	E	B	I	K
H	C	R	I	N	T	R	P	N	A
L	A	O	O	S	A	E	I	T	L
E	N	T	M	L	T	D	N	E	F
G	D	C	L	E	S	M	E	R	W
N	L	G	I	F	T	A	A	U	O
A	E	N	A	M	W	O	N	S	N
R	E	I	N	D	E	E	R	S	S

ANGEL
BERRY
CANDLE
CAROLS
CHRISTMAS
COMET
DECEMBER
GIFT
HAT
PINE
RED
REINDEER
RIBBON
SNOWFLAKE
SNOWMAN
WINTER

Find the words (from the list) in the word search to figure out the mystery word!

Extra pictures for your nativity scenes!

Extra pictures!

Bonus: Cut out the puzzle pieces. Then glue the nativity puzzle pieces on another sheet of paper.

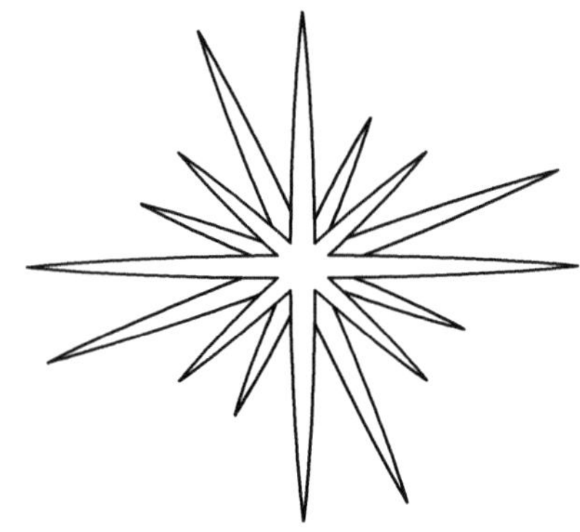

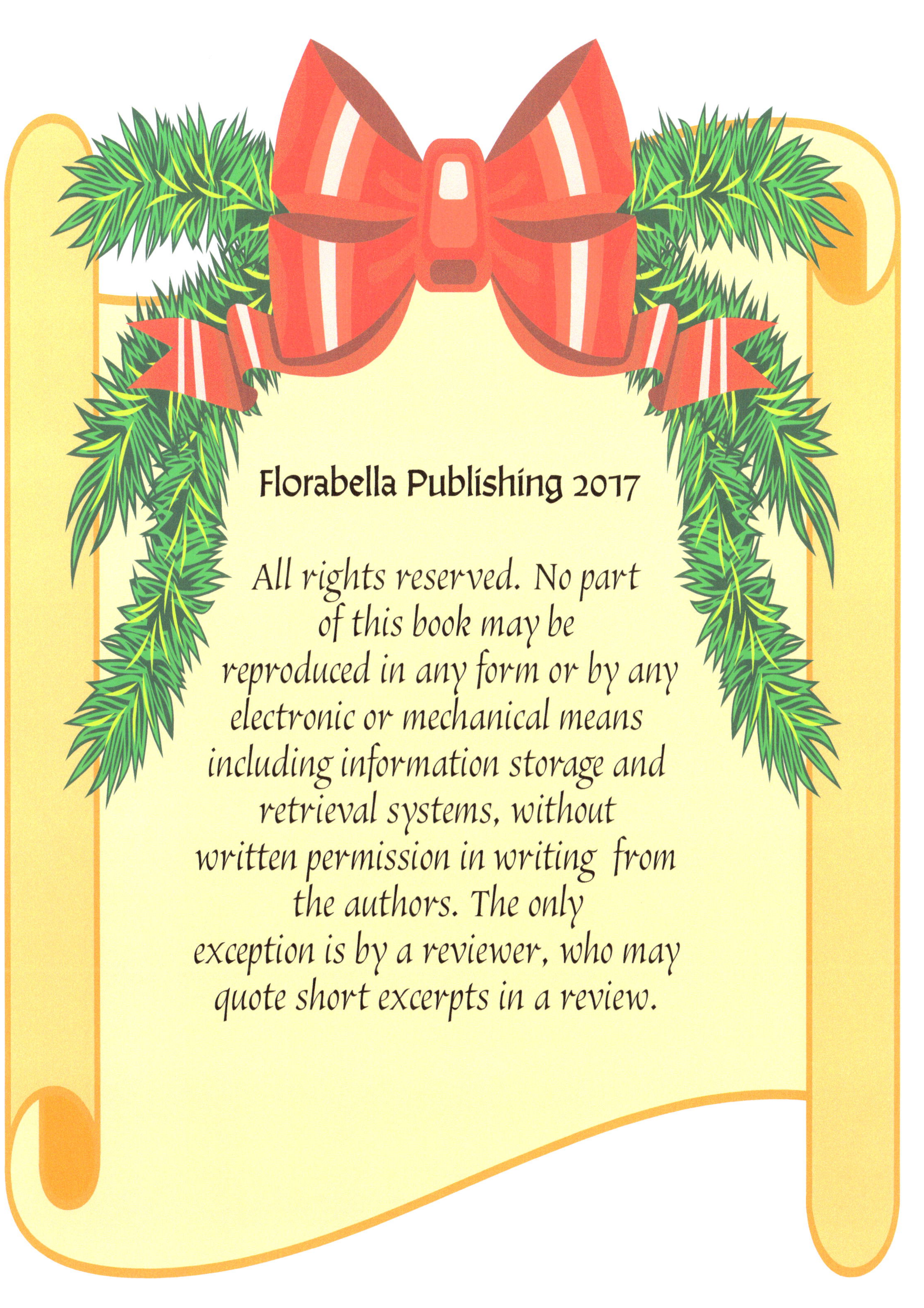

EMMA,
May Your Christmas
Be Merry & Bright!

Florabella Publishing, LLC
florabellapublishing.com